WRITERS IN Scotland

FIONA NORRIS

Hodder & Stoughton

A MEMBER OF THE HODDER HEADLINE GROUP

British Library Cataloguing in Publication Data
A catalogue for this title is available from the British Library.

ISBN 0 340 61871 X

First published 1994
Impression number   10 9 8 7 6 5 4 3 2 1
Year   1999 1998 1997 1996 1995 1994

Typeset by Wearset, Boldon, Tyne and Wear
Printed in Great Britain for Hodder & Stoughton Educational, a division of Hodder Headline Plc, 338 Euston Road, London NW1 3BH by St. Edmundsbury Press, Bury St. Edmunds, Suffolk.

Contents

Introduction

We all, as teachers of English, want our pupils to be able to talk about writing – both their own, and other people's – with some measure of confidence. The problem is often one of resources: group discussion usually is most productive when it has a structured framework on which to hang ideas, and busy teachers often look to commercially produced materials to provide that framework.

I was clear about the kind of materials I wanted – having used visiting writers in the classroom, I was aware of the value to pupils of having a 'real' writer to talk about their work. The problem, of course, was financial – there just wasn't enough money to have writers in the classroom as often as I wanted. So really what was needed was a video of writers talking about their work, about the whole process of putting words on paper. Certainly something like this existed already – but it was completely exclusive of Scottish writers, and, moreover, did not approach the kind of simplicity and depth I was after.

So it was that the video 'Writers in Scotland' came about. Three writers, **Alan Spence**, **Janice Galloway** and **Brian McCabe**, talk about the process of writing; the video is structured around eight areas of interest, so that teachers may look at just one area, or use the whole video as a stimulus to discussion.

The materials contained here are designed to complement the video: not so much 'follow up' as 'work with' materials, their aim is to enable pupils to discuss aspects of writing, and then to experiment with writing of their own. It is assumed the students will be working in small groups and the materials address pupils directly.

PART ONE contains discussion questions which explore each of the eight sections included in the video; for each section there are some quotations from the text of the video, points for discussion and suggestions for developing students' writing.

PART TWO enables students to examine a complete text by each of the three writers and to write about it if they wish.

Finally, for any students who may have had their appetite whetted, there is a suggested list of further reading into which they might delve.

These materials are designed to be of practical use to classroom teachers trying to help pupils towards a meaningful discussion of the process of writing and to save teachers a bit of time. I hope you find that they do.

Fiona Norris

PART ONE

Beginnings

**Your discussion is going to explore the idea of 'Beginnings',
both your own first experiences of writing, and also the very
practical problem of how you actually begin to put words on
paper. First of all, read the brief comments by writers Alan
Spence, Janice Galloway and Brian McCabe: their words
might help you to formulate your own ideas. Then, use the
questions provided as a framework for your discussion, but
remember that these questions are designed to stimulate
your thoughts – there are no 'right' answers!**

First Experiences

'I had grown up in Glasgow, in Govan, in fact, which wasn't the
most beautiful part of the planet, and kind of looking around for
things to write about. I couldn't see much further than what was
in front of my nose. You know, I remember looking out of the
window one time, and feeling a wee bit cheated in comparison
with folk like Dylan Thomas in terms of what they had to write
about, and it was one of these wee moments of revelation where I
thought, no, this is what you've got to write about: you know, the
tenements and the middens and the wine drinkers and scabby
dugs and the housing schemes.'

Alan Spence

'I think all children write. I think very young children like to write
and of course I, like all young children, liked to write stories . . .
but I think that there is a thing that where you come from does to
you, and a thing that maybe even parents do to you and a thing
that your friends do to you that makes you think that writing is
somehow attached to a purpose that is academic, it is attached to
exams, in other words if it is not attached to exams it's somehow
playing about or fooling yourself or it is something almost to be
embarrassed about.'

Janice Galloway

1. Think about your first experiences of writing. What kind of things did you write? How old were you? Did you write at home or school? How did you feel about writing then?

2. What do you think is 'the thing' which Janice Galloway talks about? How does it stop you writing?

3. How do you feel about the writing which you are asked to do in school? Do you enjoy it? Can you think of anything which might make it easier or more enjoyable for you?

4. Do you ever write just for yourself? What do you write – poems? Stories? Plays?

5. Why do you think so many people are embarrassed to admit that they write poems?

6. What kind of thing do you tend to write *about*? Can you see any way of using what Alan Spence has said to help your own writing?

Putting Pen to Paper

'I do carry a notebook about and I do make notes. I love being on buses, I get great ideas on buses, just looking out the windows, getting snapshots of things as they pass by, anything that strikes me as exciting or interesting or even if it strikes me as intensely boring, if it is unusual in its intensity I write it down; so if I am stuck, if I am not sure what to write about I will get this book.'

Janice Galloway

'I've written poems in response to things I've read in the newspaper. I think you have to have a response to something. If it's a memory you're starting from it has to be a memory that you yourself are intrigued by, that you yourself are wondering about, or maybe it's a peculiarly vivid memory.'

Brian McCabe

'I just jot down things that I think I'm going to bring into the story as it goes along and then it's a case of just getting that first sentence down on paper and then the next sentence and on like that, just see where it leads, and at the right point these wee things that are jotted down will find a way to come in, I'll see a way of incorporating them into the story, or maybe not, maybe something I've jotted down will go out the window. It won't add to the story or it might be in a first draft and then it'll get ditched at a later stage. It's almost like making a piece of music.'

Alan Spence

1. **What do you think of Janice Galloway's 'notebook' idea? Can you think of any other ways of recording observations?**

2. **What are the advantages of using newspaper articles as a springboard for your own writing?**

3. **What do you think Alan Spence means when he compares writing to 'making a piece of music'?**

Developing Your Writing

You might like to try one or more of the following ideas for stimulating writing. It can be helpful to share ideas and responses with someone else, or with a group.

1. **Imagine that you are looking out of a window – it can be one of the windows of your house, or a school window, or the window of a bus. Write down, in note form first of all, what you 'see'. Then try to shape your notes into a coherent piece of writing.**

2. **Look at a newspaper and pick out an article to which you have a strong response. What does it make you feel – anger? Fear? Sadness? Write a reply of some sort to the article, in any way you choose.**

3. Try keeping a writer's 'notebook' for a week. Write down anything which strikes you as being funny, or sad, or just unusual in some way. You don't have to write much – just a few words might be enough. At the end of the week, pick one of your observations and use it to begin a piece of writing.

Using Personal Experience

Your discussion is going to explore the idea of using personal experience in your writing. First of all, before you read or discuss anything, take 10 or 15 minutes and think back to your early childhood. Make a brief note of any incident or object – a special event, an argument, a gift – which comes to mind. There's no need to write much: a few sentences, or even just an image, will do. When everyone in the group is ready, read the brief comments by writers Alan Spence, Brian McCabe and Janice Galloway: their words might help you to formulate your own ideas. Then, use the questions provided as a framework for your discussion, but remember that these questions are designed to stimulate *your* thoughts – there are no 'right' answers!

'I saw Alastair Gray being interviewed on T.V. one time about "Lanark" and the interviewer asked him if it was autobiographical and Alastair said "Yes, but distorted" and that just sums it up beautifully: it's what you do, you take your own experience and you shape it and you change it, muck around with it and it was a tremendous eye opener to me to realize that I could use my own experience in a piece of writing, that my own experience was just as valid as anybody else's that had ever written.'

Alan Spence

'I think most of my stories are a mixture of experience, whether it is personal experience or not, something drawn from life and something made up, something imagined. So I mean sometimes I start from a kind of imaginative or fictional beginning. I will have a character or a situation and I am not sure where that comes from, it comes from the subconscious mind maybe; and then I will maybe draw on, not necessarily personal experience but experience of people, of life, to try and make that realistic, to try and make it seem real for a reader. At other times it happens the other way around and I will start from something drawn from life and it moves more into fiction. It is not usually a very simple process because I think when you start to describe a memory you have to start inventing right away.'

Brian McCabe

'It is astonishing how many people seem to think that if a science-fiction writer writes about little purple people on the planet Coursben it somehow means he made it all up. This is mince! You cannot make something up that you cannot make up. In other words, it's come out of something in their life, and the way these little people behave toward each other will be the way they think people behave towards each other. It doesn't matter what your characters are or where the setting is, it all comes out of your interpretation of what it is to be alive!'

Janice Galloway

1. **'When you start to describe a memory you have to start inventing right away.'**

   This statement by Brian McCabe almost looks like a contradiction in terms, doesn't it – how can a memory be 'invented'? What do you think he means here? At what point in the process of describing a memory might 'inventing' begin?

2. **How does this connect with what Alan Spence says about 'distorting' your own experience in writing?**

3. **What is Janice Galloway saying about the connections between a writer's experience of life and what is written?**

Is this a *surprising* view of fiction? How do you usually think of fiction?

4. Alan Spence talks about the moment when he realized that his experience was just as valid as anyone else's, that it was okay to write about himself, his experience. How encouraged do you feel to write about your own experience? Have you ever felt that you weren't really *qualified* to write? What made you feel like that? (Books? School? Parents? Friends?) Can you think of anything, any measure which might be taken, which would make you feel more confident about writing?

5. Turn now to the childhood memory which you briefly recorded before this discussion. Each member of the group will tell the others the memory; when each individual is finished speaking, the others will ask brief questions to try to help the speaker remember more detail. (For example, you might ask the speaker what he/she was wearing at the time, what they were feeling, what they thought other people were feeling, what the weather was like – anything to jog their memory.) However, if anyone feels that their memory is too painful to relate, or just too private, they should not be forced to speak. Move on to the next person – remember, the point of the exercise is to help and encourage each other.

Developing Your Writing

You might like to try one or more of the following ideas for stimulating writing. It can be helpful to share ideas and responses with someone else, or with a group.

1. Look at the 'memory' you have jotted down so far: can you add anything to it? Do any images, or words, or feelings, come to mind? Note them down – it doesn't matter if they seem unconnected at first, you may only

make connections later. When you have done that, begin to write. It may be that you have already decided on the form of the piece – a poem, a story, a piece of script – and if so, fine, go ahead. If you haven't, try just writing a paragraph or two, and see if the form suggests itself.

2. Think about a person who has been significant in your life, and try to describe the person and your relationship with him/her. It may be helpful to write about how the person makes you *feel*, before you try anything more detailed.

3. Think of the last time you felt really happy – one of those times when it feels great to be alive. Describe the feeling and what gave rise to it in as much detail as you can.

Developing Ideas

Your discussion is going to explore the way that ideas are developed in writing: firstly, the process of working with your ideas in writing; and secondly how you go about editing your writing. First of all, read the brief comments by writers Janice Galloway, Alan Spence and Brian McCabe: their words might help you to formulate your own ideas. Then, use the questions provided as a framework for your discussion, but remember that these questions are designed to stimulate *your* thoughts – there are no 'right' answers!

What Does it Mean?

'I start where I start and I steer the story until it gets somewhere. What was the beginning may be cut off later, but I only know how to move in a kind of logical progression through a story. That and keeping the foot down, just keeping writing what happens next, feeling when I have run out of things to say that are interesting about that particular thing that that is where it stops. It is very important for me not to try and resolve issues, that is another literary convention; it is just so stupid, life never resolves issues very well.'

Janice Galloway

'I don't sit down consciously to write a story which will make a particular religious or social point, you know. I just start to write a story and most things that are inside me that demand articulation find a way of being expressed in that particular mode or story or play or poem. I think that's what makes it interesting, that you don't know quite exactly what's going to be in the story when you start writing it. Otherwise, I think it would be turgid, it would be mechanical, there wouldn't be any sense of discovery in it for the writer. It has to be something that's unfolding out as you're going along. And even though maybe, you know, as I say, some of the surface details of a story might be in my head when I start – I might know that that moment is coming at the end, these wee motifs and things are going to surface – what the story's really actually about is something that becomes clear to me in the writing of it.'

Alan Spence

'Sometimes I'll kind of hang a story on a central image – for instance the story I wrote called "The Full Moon" is about a man working in a therapy unit of a mental hospital and in this story he's making a moon out of cardboard and golden paper. He sees his face reflected in this golden moon he's making and it's distorted, and one side of the moon is painted black. At the time of writing the story I didn't obviously think, ah this is a symbolic moon which means X, but I was aware that it was, it did seem to be meaning more than just what it was, just a kind of decoration, just an object. So I think when you're using an image like that or a symbol in a poem or a story, you have to have faith in it in a way. I think if you question it as a writer, if you say, what does this mean? you undermine it really.'

Brian McCabe

1. It is often said that a story has to have a beginning, a middle and an end. How does that affect the way you *plan* a story, what you decide before you begin to write?

2. Does what these writers say about how they develop ideas in their stories surprise you? Is this the way *you* work?

3. What does Janice Galloway mean when she says that 'life never resolves issues very well'? How does this affect the way you might *end* a story?

4. What does Alan Spence mean when he says that a story has to have a 'sense of discovery in it for the writer'? If you were working like this, how would it affect any plan you might have made at the outset?

5. Look at what Brian McCabe says about having faith in an image – do you understand what he means when he says this? Do *you* always feel that you have to have an explanation for using a particular image in your writing?

The Editing Process

'I would say it is a guarantee that the editing process should be at least three times as long as the creative process if your story is going to be any good, if it isn't going to be a kind of sick-up onto the page.'

Janice Galloway

'I tend to work fairly slowly, so in a sense my rewriting is happening as I go along. I've already maybe rewritten something before it gets down and that sounds crazy! I've worked through it in my head to an extent where the words going down on the page are the right words as far as I can make them the right words and when I'm going back over things it tends to be fairly small adjustments I'm making, you know, take out a paragraph here or change a bit of punctuation there.'

Alan Spence

'I ask friends to look at things I'm writing sometimes, especially if it's something that I'm having trouble with, something that isn't working. It often helps to let someone else see what you're writing because other people can sometimes just see more quickly what should be down here or what's not working and who is not working because you yourself, you're the writer of the piece so you'll sometimes get too close to it to see certain things.'

Brian McCabe

1. **Clearly, it is possible to edit your material in different ways. Describe how *you* go about redrafting a piece of writing.**

2. **When you're redrafting, are you just looking for surface errors (spelling and punctuation mistakes, for example) or do you actually change what happens in the story, or the way you're telling it?**

   What do you think should be the purpose of redrafting?

3. **Do you ever ask someone else to read a first draft? (If so, who? If not, why not?)**

4. **Would you rather have an early draft looked at by a friend, or by a teacher? (The two, of course, are not mutually exclusive!)**

   Do you think they would look at the work in different ways?

   What kind of comment is *most* helpful to you?

   What kind of comment is *least* helpful to you?

Developing Your Writing

You might like to try one or more of the following ideas in your writing. It can be helpful to share ideas and responses with someone else, or with a group.

Here is a list of images, brief 'snapshots': choose one which appeals to you and use it in a piece of writing. You might find it helpful to think about the image first, before jotting down words, phrases and ideas which seem to you to be associated with it.

(a) **A bunch of white carnations.**
(b) **Red drops on a black stone.**
(c) **A woman walking slowly, with an empty pram.**
(d) **A yellow room with a chair, a bed, an open window.**

Exploring the Mind of a Child

Your discussion is going to focus on the way in which we use children in writing, both as subjects in stories, poems and plays, and as a vehicle for exploring the child who lives in all of us. First of all, read the brief comments by writers Janice Galloway, Brian McCabe and Alan Spence: their words might help you to formulate your own ideas. Then, use the questions provided as a framework for your discussion, but remember that these questions are designed to stimulate *your* thoughts – there are no 'right' answers!

'There is no more important thing to look at in the world than how adults treat kids and how kids are helped to think about themselves in the world, because as adults all they are is big kids. Remember being wee and thinking, when I'm grown up I'll be like this and I'll be like that and I'll have control of this and I'll know about this? Nobody ever tells you, you just get more birthdays, that's all that happens, you're actually just the same inside.'

Janice Galloway

'I think I am interested in explaining the mind of a child in some poems and some stories because it does offer a kind of freedom for me as a writer. For a start it allows me to get away from conventional adult perfections and I am quite interested in exploring what a child's imagination can do, so I wrote one story in which a boy is put outside the door of a classroom at school and he's mentally talking to an imaginary friend from Mars. In another story a young boy picks up a stone from a path he's walking along and he starts wondering what it would be like to be a stone and this leads him onto wondering what it would be like to be dead. I think sometimes a child's mind can just open up a lot of important issues from a different angle.'

Brian McCabe

'Everything's absolutely total when you're a kid and as people get older they tend to close down more and settle for things, settle for a particular role in life, a role in society, and maybe that clarity of perception gets dulled somewhat, you know, folk get weighted down with responsibilities and burdened. So I think when folk are remembering their own childhood they're remembering that clarity and that intensity and that vividness that's there when you're a kid. And also it's an attempt, I think, to understand how you've become what you are as an adult.'

Alan Spence

1. **How much do you think *you* have changed from the small child you were? How have your perceptions of the world changed?**

2. **Children often have a strong belief in 'magic' of various kinds (e.g. Santa Claus, ghosts, the tooth fairy) which eventually disappears as they begin to understand reality. Can you talk about a moment when you realized that something in which you believed did not exist, was not 'magical' at all?**

3. **What do you think Brian McCabe means when he talks about 'conventional adult perfections'? Can you think of any examples?**

4. **Look at what Alan Spence says about children's 'clarity of perception'. What do you understand this to mean? Can**

you think of any examples of times when a child's perception might be *clearer* than that of an adult?

5. Can you think of any occasions when adults deliberately lie to children? (Why do they do this – to protect them?)

6. Adults often think of children as 'innocent' – do you think this is true? Do you think that adults *need* to believe in the essential 'innocence' of childhood?

Developing Your Writing

1. Think back to the moment when you discovered that something 'magical' did not exist at all. Write in any way you wish about the experience and the feelings it evoked.

2. Many children have imaginary 'friends': write a conversation which a child might have with one such friend.

3. Children often *trust* adults completely. Think about a time when you felt let down or betrayed by an adult and write about it; again, concentrate on remembering the feelings you had at the time.

4. Children often interpret adult instructions very literally – sometimes with comic results. Write a story, or a poem, which uses this idea.

Genre

Your discussion is going to explore the different *forms* of writing and the challenges they present. First of all, read the brief comments by writers Janice Galloway, Alan Spence and Brian McCabe: their words might help you to formulate your own ideas. Then, use the questions provided as a framework for your discussion, but remember that these questions are designed to stimulate *your* thoughts – there are no 'right' answers!

'Starting to write a novel is wonderful because you have everything open in front of you; the most obvious difference between short stories and a novel – a novel is a big bit of writing that is all joined up and short stories are little bits of writing that are not necessarily all joined up. The big bit is great when it starts because you are opening up possibilities, you are raising questions all the time, anything is open to you. The horror starts when you are about a third of the way through, you have got another 200 pages still to keep going, you hit a desert. Two-thirds of the way through you hit a black hole in the middle of the desert and you think, who is going to read this rubbish anyway. It is very, very trying, you need an awful lot of self-confidence just to push yourself through it and it is not talent that writes a novel in the end, the talent helps it to be a good novel, but the only thing that ever got a novel written was persistence.'

Janice Galloway

'I found it very liberating writing a play for the first time, just working with other folk, for instance, working with a director, with actors, seeing how the thing could be fluid and change. You tend to, you know, if you're working on a story or poem, write it and it's finished and that's it, you've done it; it goes into print and it's done. You write a play and that's just the start of it, you know, the director takes that draft and mucks around with it and suggests changes and you argue with him and you agree with him on some points and the whole thing starts to change and shift and become something different altogether, and then it goes into rehearsals and the actors put their input in and it changes again.'

Alan Spence

'I think short stories are very different from novels because in a novel you've got room to have lots of different events, lots of different characters, different time scales and you can move around a lot, you might have more than one there on the go. In a short story, in my short stories at least, I tend to focus on something quite closely and emphatically and it might just be one event or one moment in someone's life.'

Brian McCabe

1. What kind of writing – poetry, stories, plays – are you most asked to write in class? (If *one* of these forms of writing tends to dominate, can you think why?)

2. What kind of writing do you *prefer*?

3. Are you afraid of tackling a particular form of writing? If so, why? What difficulties do you associate with it?

4. Look at what Janice Galloway says about the sheer slog of writing a novel – is that what you imagined writing a novel would be like? (Or did you think that writers simply waited for 'inspiration' to fuel their pens?)

5. Sometimes, we think of writers' words as being sacrosanct, unchangeable: how does what Alan Spence says about the process of creating a play alter that idea?

6. Would it be possible to create a play in class in this way? How could you overcome any difficulties?

Developing Your Writing

You might like to try one or more of the following ideas in your writing. It can be helpful to share ideas and responses with someone else, or with a group.

1. Think about what Brian McCabe has said about creating a story around just *one* moment or event in someone's life. Choose a moment from your own life, or from the list of 'imagined' moments below, and write a story about it.

    (a) A child witnesses the death of an animal.
    (b) A teenager discovers that a parent is fallible.

(c) **An adult faces the death of a parent.**

(d) **A child is left alone in the house.**

2. **Write a short play which includes a family argument, using no more than four characters. When you have finished the first draft, ask some friends to perform it and suggest improvements. (Listen carefully to the words – do they sound natural for the character?)**

3. **Look at Brian McCabe's 'Big Sister' poems in the second section of this book: write a poem in reply to one of these, from the point of view of the younger child.**

Voices

Your discussion is going to explore the importance of the way words *sound* in writing. Before you read or discuss, though, take 10 minutes or so to jot down a sequence of words which you like the sound of, words which you enjoy saying out loud. It might be a few lines of poetry, some dialogue from a film, or something much more mundane – an advertising jingle, perhaps. When everyone in the group is ready, read the brief comments by writers Alan Spence, Janice Galloway and Brian McCabe: their words might help you to formulate your own ideas. Then, use the questions provided as a framework for your discussion, but remember that these questions are designed to stimulate *your* thoughts – there are no 'right' answers!

'I think there's a sense in which you can often spot what's wrong with a piece by hearing it – if you're faking it in some way or if you're avoiding the issue or if you're not being true in a piece of writing. Interestingly, I can always hear it in the rhythm, you know, if I'm reading something and I get the urge to rush past a wee bit, you know, maybe I should stop and look at that because it's not quite right, and if the rhythm's not right then that's usually a reflection of some deeper malaise in the story, something that's not quite truthful or just not working properly. The ear is really important to me, the music of it.'

Alan Spence

'People do say strange things all the time: people talk in half-sentences, people come out with words you would not expect them to come out with and sentiments you would not expect them to come out with. Sometimes people come out with the most baroque and poeticised language and are totally unconscious of it unless you point it out to them. To me the important thing is to listen for that, never point it out to them because they might stop doing it, and write it down. So it is important to me to try and make speech, not to play an academic game and try and make speech always consistent. People are inconsistent and hearing that voice, as long as I can hear a voice saying it I'm perfectly happy with it.'

Janice Galloway

'I'm interested in using speech and trying to capture real speech, so I'm fairly particular about how I write dialogue. I think that dialogue shouldn't be just a kind of decoration, and it shouldn't just be there to break up the description. I think dialogue at its best should be quite a purposive thing. One thing is that it should reveal character, so if you have good dialogue in a way you don't need as much character description. At the same time I think, you know, the reader has to see characters. A writer has to try and show the reader the character who is speaking, so you're going to need some description as well, some sensory description. But dialogue I think should also move the story on, it should be a dynamic thing so that part of the narration is actually taking place through the dialogue.'

Brian McCabe

1. **Look at what Alan Spence says about the 'music' of language. In what way can language be said to be like music?**

2. Janice Galloway talks about *making* speech, speech that sounds real to her; something that real people might say. Are there any problems associated with making speech sound *real* in a story?

   What do you understand by 'people are inconsistent'? How does that affect how you might represent what they say in a story?

3. What does Brian McCabe mean when he says that 'dialogue shouldn't be just a kind of decoration'?

   In what ways can dialogue 'move the story on'?

4. Do you think it's possible to 'see' characters without the descriptive element Brian McCabe talks about?

5. Look now at the words you have all jotted down: one at a time, each member of the group should talk to the others about the words, and why the *sound* of them is attractive. In your subsequent discussion you might want to consider the following:

   (a) Is the *rhythm* of the words unusual? 'Catchy' in some way?

   (b) Have linguistic devices been used to make the words memorable (e.g. alliteration, assonance, rhyme)?

   (c) Would you expect to hear these words in the course of normal conversation, or are they very literary? (Does this make them more, or less, attractive?)

Developing Your Writing

You might like to try one or more of the following ideas for stimulating writing. It can be helpful to share ideas and responses with someone else, or with a group.

1. Write a monologue, in which a character talks about him/herself: concentrate on making the character reveal him/herself through what is said.

2. **Write a short piece which involves a confrontation between two people, and which includes dialogue. Think about what the characters are feeling, and how you will convey this in writing.**

3. **Think about ways of using description, sensory detail and dialogue: write a short piece in which a character walks into a room, visibly affecting other people in that room. Aim to use both dialogue and descriptive detail.**

Character

Your discussion is going to explore the idea of character – where ideas for characters come from, and how they develop in a story. First of all, read the brief comments by writers Brian McCabe, Janice Galloway and Alan Spence: their words might help to formulate your own ideas. Then, use the questions provided as a framework for your discussion, but remember that these questions are designed to stimulate *your* thoughts – there are no 'right' answers!

'I wrote one novel called "The Other McCoy" and this began really just from the vague idea of a character who likes to impersonate people, who likes to mimic people, so I just fancied writing about a character who can't help doing this and the character grew up from that.'

Brian McCabe

'The most important thing to me is making people complex. Don't ever try to make this person the retired colonel with the gruff voice who's really got a heart of gold, who gives all the kids sweeties at the play park. I'm not interested in that kind of stereotyping. People are very complex and there are always unpleasant things in with the pleasant things, there are always contradictions, there are always times when these people do not understand themselves, and the important thing about making a character work on the page for me is to make them as inexplicable as other people are in real life. . . . For example, ways people behave when they think they are all alone and nobody's looking at them, that's the kind of thing I want to write about, the inexplicables, the strange things.'

Janice Galloway

'I remember talking to Tom McGrath, the playwright, who was writing a play about Laurel and Hardy and was completely engrossed in writing a draft when someone came to see him, and he couldn't see him because at that particular point in time he was Stan Laurel and the guy had come to see Tom McGrath, not Stan Laurel, so he had to actually tell his secretary to send the guy away and he would see him later. It is a curious aspect of writers' personalities, I think. It's to do with identifying, you're identifying with the characters you're creating to such an extent that you kind of become them, you see through their eyes, you get inside them and see out from the inside. I think it's the only way the characters are going to become real to be honest.'

Alan Spence

1. **What do you understand by 'character stereotyping'? (Look at what Janice Galloway says about it.) Can you think of any kinds of novel or story which seem deliberately to use character stereotyping? What might be the advantages of writing these kinds of characters?**

2. **Why does Janice Galloway try to avoid character stereotyping? What effect then, is she trying to achieve in her writing?**

3. **Can you think of any difficulties which might present themselves in a story in which characters are as inexplicable as people are in real life? (*Is* a story 'real life'?)**

4. **Do you find Alan Spence's anecdote about Tom McGrath 'becoming' Stan Laurel surprising? Have you ever had an**

experience like that? What about when you were a small child, making up stories while playing? Did you ever 'become' Superman etc? Can you see a link between the way children involve themselves in their stories, and the process of creating a character?

5. In what sense does a character 'become real' when a writer identifies with him or her?

6. How would this process of identification enable a character to 'grow' in a story?

7. 'Sometimes I will invent a character that I think is in a dreadful bad mood at the start of a story and then when I show it to somebody else they'll say, "I really liked her, I mean, she was just so sad" and I'll say "What do you mean she was sad, she was meant to be really crabbit, you're not meant to like her".'

Janice Galloway

How does the way the *reader* interacts with the character help a character to 'grow'?

Can you make a summarising statement about the strange, triangular relationship between writer, character and reader?

Developing Your Writing

You might like to try one or more of the following ideas for stimulating writing. It can be helpful to share ideas and responses with someone else, or with a group.

1. Invent a character who has one very unusual characteristic; write everything you can about the character, including a physical description.

2. Write about one day in the life of a character – you may wish to choose someone who seems to you to be very

ordinary (a housewife, a bus conductor) or someone who
is extraordinary.

3. Choose a person who interests you, from history or
   mythology, and imagine that you *are* that person. Write
   an episode – real or imagined – in their life.

The Scottish Dimension

Your discussion is going to explore the idea of 'Scottishness'
in writing, the importance of nationality in what you write.
Before you begin, take five minutes to jot down the names of
any Scottish writers whose works you have enjoyed. Then,
read the brief comments by writers Alan Spence and Janice
Galloway: their words might help you to formulate your own
ideas. Finally, use the questions provided as a framework for
your discussion, but remember that these questions are
designed to stimulate *your* thoughts – there are no 'right'
answers!

'There's a certain rhythm that is in my prose that, you know, is in
other Glasgow writers' prose. It is very distinctly West of Scotland
and has a kind of energy because of that. It was a conscious
decision to explore that when I started writing stories, as it was
for Tom Leonard writing his poetry for instance. We were seeing
what you could do with this spoken language that we heard round
about us with its rhythms, with its energy and its humour. So I
suppose I was aware of myself being Glaswegian even, rather than
Scottish. Scottish was kilts and White Heather Club and all that,
whereas Glasgow was where I'd grown up. I think there's a lot to
be gained by exploring these roots that we have, you know, and
just start with where you are.'

Alan Spence

'It is not important to be "Scottish" because that would be putting
it on like a jumper, you know – like it is important to be warm

and I put this piece of clothing on; it is important to be Scottish, so I am going to be it. I have no choice: I am. If I had a choice, who knows what I might have done, but we none of us have a choice, you are born where you are born and it does things to you, just as you were born to the people you were born to, and they do things to you. There is no getting round that; that is why class matters, not because class is a big issue but because you were born to certain people who taught you certain things were your limitations and certain things were your expectations; you were born in a geographical location which likewise taught you, because of the social ethos which surrounds that country, that certain things are your limitations and certain things are your expectations. The important thing is always to be asking questions and breaking expectations, but unless you know what the expectations you were dumped with in the first place are, you are going to find that job much more difficult. So the Scottishness matters insofar as that is where I begin, but it is certainly not an objective, it is certainly not something that I am moving through in order to prove a point, it just happens to be my place in the landscape: that is where I was born – female, working-class, Scottish. That's it. I have got three feet.'

Janice Galloway

1. **What does Alan Spence mean when he differentiaties between the Scotland represented by 'kilts and White Heather Club and all that' and the place where he grew up?**

   Can you think of any other examples of the kilts/White Heather Club representation of 'Scottishness'?

2. **Is this idea at variance with your own feeling of what it is to be Scottish?**

3. '. . . you were born in a geographical location which likewise taught you, because of the social ethos which surrounds that country, that certain things are your limitations and certain things are your expectations.'

   Janice Galloway

What 'social ethos' is connected with Scotland? Does this vary *within* Scotland? (Is there a difference between rural/urban Scotland? Or Highland/Lowland Scotland?)

4. Look now at the brief list of Scottish writers you have jotted down:

    (a) Why do you like these writers/books?

    (b) Look at Alan Spence's comment on the rhythms in his writing – is there anything he says which seems applicable to any of these writers?

    N.B. If you can't think of any Scottish writers you have enjoyed, you might like to try some of the works listed at the end of Part Two.

5. Look at the following statement by Janice Galloway and discuss to what extent you agree with it.

'I am sad to say that there is a kind of South-East mafia who for a long time have been awarding each other literary prizes, who tend to look on Scotland as, "Well, it's north of the border really, isn't it?" It's "Well, Scottish writers write for Scottish people; who else could they be writing for? Who else wants to know what is happening in Glasgow or Aberdeen? Who else knows where these places are?"'

For additional information, you might like to look through some of the national 'qualities', e.g. the Times, Guardian, Observer and note how many of the books they review are by Scottish writers.

Developing Your Writing

You might like to try writing about one or more of the following issues which will have arisen in your discussion; you may wish to write a response which is in a fictional form, or you may wish to write an opinion piece.

1. 'Writers in Scotland are writing for the Scots.' To what extent is this statement accurate?

2. 'You are born where you are born and it does things to you.' Write about where you were born.

3. 'Scottish was kilts and White Heather Club and all that.' What does 'Scottish' mean to you?

Brian McCabe

Brian McCabe was born in a small mining community near Edinburgh. His father worked as a coal miner, his mother as a cook. He studied philosophy and English literature at the University of Edinburgh. Since 1980 he has lived as a freelance writer. He has published two volumes of poetry, 'Spring's Witch' (Mariscat, 1984) and 'One Atom to Another' (Polygon, 1987); a collection of short stories 'The Lipstick Circus' (Mainstream, 1985). All three won Scottish Arts Council Book Awards. His novel 'The Other McCoy' (Mainstream/Penguin) was published in 1990. He lives in Edinburgh with his family and is currently Writer in Residence for Ross and Cromarty.

His most recent book is a collection of short stories 'In a Dark Room with a Stranger' (Hamish Hamilton, 1993/Penguin, 1994).

The Big Sister Poems

THE MESSAGE

Little brother I got a message for you
not from Santa no
it's from Da.
Listen will you.

See before you got born
see Da still had a job to do.
We got bacon and eggs for breakfast.
Ma used to afford to get a hair-do.

Then she goes and gets pregnant again
and even although it was by accident
Da said we could maybe still afford it.
He meant you.

It turns out we can't.

The other thing is
this room before you came along
only had the one bed in it.
Mine.

See there isn't really room for the two.
So what with one thing and another
and since you were the last to arrive
Da says you've to go little brother.

Here is your bag it's packed ready
with your Beanos pyjamas and a few
biscuits for when you get hungry
I'm sure you'll be better off wherever

you end up so good luck and
goodbye.

A BEDTIME STORY

There was a bottle with a dream in it.
Da drank from it because
this dream made everything seem
a lot better than they was.

A boring word sounded cleverer
and like it might mean more
and even his jokes sounded funnier
than they ever been before.

The dream it made Da swagger
and laugh and drink up more
till swagger turned into stagger
and laugh turned into roar.

Then the dream turned into a bad dream
and it made Da curse and swore.
So when he got back home at last
well he banged the front door.

See Da in this dream is someone
who knows when he's always right
so when Ma went and argued with him
they started to shout and fight.

They fight about Da and his dreaming
see then the nightmare goes on
he's hitting her now she's screaming
then this morning Ma's gone.

And Da says he can't remember
what the dream was all about.
So he goes out to look for her.
Don't ask me how I found this out.

I'm yer big sister amn't I.
I know things you don't that's all.
Like the story of the bottle with a dream in it
a dream called that's right.

now get to sleep.

THE LESSON

I'll tell you what now little brother
I'm going to teach you something
you'll never ever forget.

You go half way upstairs that's right.
You turn round you shut your eyes.
You keep them shut tight.

Now on the count of five
now I want you to jump.
Now is that clear.

Don't be scared little brother.
I'll be standing at the bottom here
to catch you so be brave.

1 . . . 2 . . . 3 . . . 4 . . .

Five I said I'd teach you something
this is it don't ever trust anybody.
When you're older you'll thank me for it.

Shut up.

THE VISITORS

Little brother you'll never guess what.
The aliens have just landed.
No they don't have pointed ears
but they are armed and handed.

No they don't have suckers.
No not red blue yellow or green.
But all in black and silver
and one keeps a talking machine.

in a special secret pocket.
You can see the blue light out there
well it comes from their rocket.
You can hear their voices downstairs

they're talking to Da that's right.
They want to know where he was
on the planet Earth last night
between seven and ten because

how should I know?
Ma says they'll go away soon
but if you ask me I don't think so.
I think they'll take Da to the moon.

No they are not friendly.
No you can't go downstairs.
I will protect you don't worry.
Move over.

THE WARNING

Little brother beware the black car
with the strangers' faces in the windows –
the one they call the Getaway Waggon
taking Da to the job he goes.

Little brother beware the black car
with the iron bars in its windows –
the one they call the Black Maria
taking Da to the jail he goes.

Little brother beware the black car
with the dark glass in all its windows –
the one they call the Funeral Hearse
taking Da to the grave he goes.

Little brother beware the black car
no matter what is in its windows
no matter what they call it
taking Da to wherever he goes.

one day it will come for you.

The Big Sister Poems

Discussion Points

The Message

1. Why does the big sister tell her brother that the 'message' is from his father?

2. She tells her brother what life was like before he arrived on the scene. What is the *tone* here?

3. Clearly, the big sister is teasing her little brother, when she says that she's packed a bag for him – but is there a serious side to her teasing?

4. What do you think is the real 'message' which the girl is trying to give her brother? (Is there any sense in which she is trying to *protect* him?)

5. If you are a sibling, are there feelings expressed in the poem with which you can identify?

6. How is the *humour* of the poem achieved?

A Bedtime Story

1. What is the frightening sequence of events which the big sister has witnessed?

2. Why does she tell her little brother about it in this roundabout way?

3. In what sense might alcohol be said to have a dream in it? Does this help to explain why the father drinks?

4. There is a terrible irony in the title of the poem – can you say what it is?

5. 'I'm yer big sister amn't I.' What does this reveal about the way the big sister feels about her little brother?

6. Try to detail the ways in which Brian McCabe manages to create the *voice* of the big sister in this poem – (What kind of *language* is used? Formal? Slang? What about the *grammar* of the sentences?)

The Lesson

1. What has actually happened in this poem?

2. What 'lesson' do you think the big sister is trying to teach her little brother?

3. What does the poem tell you about what the big sister's experience of life has been? (How 'big' do you think she is?)

4. What is the saddest aspect of this poem, for you?

The Visitors

1. Why does the big sister describe the policemen as 'aliens'? (In what sense *are* they alien to her?)

2. She describes the possibility of her father being arrested as though it were a part of a science-fiction fantasy – why? (Is it comforting for her to do so? Does it make it easier to bear?)

3. What is the effect of the *rhyme* in this poem?

The Warning

1. The 'black car' in this poem is, on one level, three different types of vehicle – but does it seem to you to symbolise anything else?

2. How is a feeling of *menace* created in this poem? (Consider the first line in each stanza and the adjectives.)

3. Look at the last line of the poem – why is it isolated? What does it mean?

4. What is 'the warning' which the big sister is giving her little brother?

Writing About the Poems

It may be that, following your discussion of these poems, you wish to explore them further by writing about them. Here are a few suggestions for you to consider – they may help you clarify your thoughts.

1. Consider the relationship between the 'big sister' and her little brother throughout the sequence of poems – how would you describe it?

   What kind of family are they part of? How does this affect the way the girl feels about her brother?

2. Think about the way the personality, the 'voice' of the sister is created throughout the poems. Consider:

   (a) Use of repetition.
   (b) The *kind* of rhyme used – what does it suggest?
   (c) The grammatical mistakes – inconsistencies of tense etc.
   (d) The use of humour.

3. Clearly, the poems deal with the loss of innocence – but whose?

Alan Spence

A poet, short story writer, novelist and playwright, Alan Spence was born in Glasgow and now lives in Edinburgh. He has published a novel, 'The Magic Flute' (Black Swan) and a collection of stories 'Its Colours They Are Fine' (Black Swan) as well as three plays, 'Sailmaker', 'Changed Days' and 'Space Invaders' (all Hodder & Stoughton).

'Nessun Dorma', the short story featured here, won the 'Scotland on Sunday' 1993 short story competition.

Nessun Dorma

It's the first thing I hear when I step out into the street, Pavarotti at full volume, belting out *Nessun Dorma*. Half past six in the morning, the streetlights on, the sky above the tenements just starting to get light. Three closes along, on the other side, the ground floor window is wide open, pushed up as far as it can go. That's where the music is coming from. It builds to its crescendo, *Vincero*. It stops. There's a brief silence. Then it starts all over again.

I peer across as I pass by, but I can't really see in. The lights are off in the house. All I can make out is a faint glow that might be from a TV in the corner. The curtains are flapping, whipped about by that freezing Edinburgh breeze, straight off the North Sea.

In the papershop at the corner, Kenny from upstairs is buying his Daily Record, his cigarettes.

'Early shift this week?' I ask him.

'That's right. It's a bugger.' He says. 'Wife still away?'

'She'll be back at the weekend. Hey, did you hear that racket in the street?'

'The music,' he says: 'that World Cup thing?'

'Pavarotti.'

'I think it's been on all night. I got in the back of ten and it was going full blast then.'

'Weird.'

'The thing is.' He has pulled open the door, set the bell above it jangling. He stands half in half out of the shop. 'I couldn't help wondering if she was okay. The wifie in the house like. I mean, I looked in the window when I was passing and she was just sitting there in the dark wi' the TV on and that music blaring out. Over and over.'

'Could be a video and she's rewinding it.'

'Aye.' He looks uncomfortable. 'Anyway. Maybe somebody should make sure she's all right. I'd do it myself but I've got my work to go to.'

'Sure.'

'So.'

'Right.'

He lets the door go and it closes behind him.

'Thanks Kenny.'

'Christ.'

Back along the street with my milk and rolls, the paper. I have to look in and see for myself. The music is still playing, louder the nearer I get. Right outside the window it's deafening. The curtains are still being tugged about by the wind, white net gone grubby. They flap out and I catch their dusty smell.

Inside, the TV flickers bright and harsh. Pavarotti is in close-up, the colours lurid and wrong, his face orange. Silhouetted in the blue light from the screen, I can make out the woman, sitting in an armchair, her back to the window. I lean right in and call out hello, above the music. My eyes adjust to the light and a few things take shape. A stack of newspapers on the table, an empty whisky bottle, ashtray full to overflowing, a carton of longlife milk. And the smell hits me, reek of drink and stale tobacco and somewhere in at the back of it a pervading sourness like old matted clothes in a jumble sale. The room stinks of misery. It's a smell I remember.

I call out hello again, hello there, and this time her head turns, she makes some kind of noise.

'Are you all right?'

She heaves herself up in the chair. She's a big woman, heavy. I recognise her, I've seen her in the street. Not old, maybe late forties, fifty. She steadies herself, peers at me blankly, takes a careful step or two towards the window. She looks terrible, her face blotched and puffy. Her hair is flattened, sticks up at the back, the way she's been leaning on it. She wears a thick wool cardigan, buttoned up, on top of what looks like a nightdress.

'What's that?' she says, looking out.

'Just making sure you're all right.'

'All right?' She has no idea who I am, what's going on. 'Yes,' she says. 'It's all right. Each one that has wronged me will come undone. Nice of you to take an interest, I would offer you a drink but it's not on. They sent for the police you know. But I told them, no uncertain terms. So now they're looking into it. Full investigation, I'll show them. Would you like a drink? No, of course. It's not on.'

She suddenly stops and looks confused, stranded in midstream. The voice of Pavarotti swells, fills the room, she lets herself be caught up in it again, lost in it. Her face crumples, folds in a grimace, a tortured smile as she stands there swaying in her stinking kitchen. The aria builds to its climax again. *Vincero.*

She finds the remote control and winds back the tape.

The Chinese dragon I painted on the wall of my room, in Glasgow, all those years ago. Eight feet long in bright, primary colours, straight onto the blank white wall.

No reason why it should come to me now, but it does. I see it floating in its swirl of cloud, fire flaring from its nostrils, its long tail curled and looped round on itself like a Celtic serpent.

The room was the first one I'd ever had completely to myself. The twenty-third floor of a highrise block. My father and I had been moved from the room and kitchen where I'd grown up, where I was born. The room and kitchen that had come to have that stink of misery I recognised just now. The smell of hopelessness, my father not coping, myself useless in the face of it.

But all that was past. The tenements were rubble and dust. We had been transported to this bright empty space high in the sky. I remember us laughing as we walked through it, shouted to each other from room to room, intoxicated by the cleanness and newness. It still smelled of fresh putty and paint. And the view from the windows had us stand there just staring. Instead of blackened tenements, the back of a factory, we could see for miles, clear down the Clyde.

I kept my room simple and uncluttered, a mattress in the corner, straw matting on the floor. And I started right away on painting that dragon. I copied it from a magazine, divided it up with a grid of squares, pencilled a bigger grid on the wall and scaled the whole thing up. That way the proportions would be right, exact. And when I'd drawn in all the lines, traced every delicate curve, I set to colouring it in, with poster-paint and a fine-tip brush.

I worked on it meticulously, a little every day, with total concentration and absolute care. After a week it was finished, except for one small section – the last few inches, the very tip of the tail. I decided to take a break over the weekend, finish it the following week. But I never did. I lived in that house for four years and never completed it. That section of tail stayed blank. When anyone asked me why, I had no idea. I just couldn't make myself pick up the brush. The dragon remained unfinished.

When I head out later along the street, Pavarotti's *bel canto* is still ringing out. *Tu pure, o Principessa nella tua fredda stanza.* Princess you too are waking in your cold room. Again that smell wafts out as I pass by.

My father had a record of *Nessun Dorma* – an old scratched 78 – sung by Jussi Bjorling. So I know the song from way back. He used to play it loud when the drink had made him maudlin, sometimes alternating it with records of mine he liked in the same way, records that moved him to tears, Edith Piaf's *Je ne regrette rien*, Joan Baez singing *Plaisir d'amour*.

In the years after my mother died, I grew to dread hearing those songs. I would stop and listen on the stairs, halfway up the dank close, knowing the state I would find him in, guttered into oblivion.

It must have been those songs that made him want to learn French.

'Got to do something about myself,' he said. 'Haul myself up by the bootstraps.'

So he'd signed up for an evening class at the university, gone along once a week.

'Give me something to look forward to,' he said.

He made lists of vocabulary in a little lined notebook.

'That tutor's some boy,' he said. 'Really knows his stuff.'

He had told the tutor he was hoping to go to France on holiday, someday.

The night I came home late and that smell hit me as soon as I opened the door. No music playing but in the quietness the hiss and steady click of the record player, the disc played out, the needle arm bobbing up and down in place. And behind that, my father breathing heavy in a deep drunken stupor. He slept in the set-in bed in the recess. I didn't want to disturb him but I wanted to turn off the record player. I switched on the light, turned and saw him.

Sprawled across the bed, still dressed, shoes on, his clothes and the bedding covered in blood, a bloodsoaked hanky wrapped round his hand.

I managed to wake him but couldn't get him up on his feet. He had drunk himself senseless, beyond all comprehension and pain, anaesthetised and numb.

I sat up all night, dozed in the chair. A couple of times he shouted out, nothing that made any sense. At first light I shook him awake, took him down to Casualty at the hospital. He had lost the tip of a finger, had no recollection where or how. The doctors stitched him up, gave him injections.

'I was on my way to the French class,' he said. 'Met a guy I used to work with, in the yards. Drinking his redundancy money. Just the one, I said. Got somewhere to go. That was it. The rest's a blur.'

'What about your hand?'

'No idea,' he said. 'Except maybe.' He stopped. 'Just a vague memory. Getting it jammed in a taxi door.'

'Where in God's name were you going in a taxi?'

'I haven't a clue, son. Haven't a clue.'

For a while after that he was ill. A low ebb. He never went back to his evening class, never finished the course. He was giving up on everything, until this move to the new place, the high rise. A fresh start.

I like to get settled in the library early, get a good stint of work done in the morning. But today I just can't seem to focus. So I'm glad of the distraction when Neil comes in, sits down at the table next to me.

'How's the mature student?' he asks. 'Working on something?'

'Dissertation,' I tell him. 'Zen in Scottish literature.'

'Wild!'

'Of all the people on the planet you're the one most likely to appreciate it.'

'Hey thanks!'

His beard and long hair are grizzled these days. The archetypal Old Hippy.

'Passed these young guys in the street the other day,' he says. 'And they're looking me up and down. And one of them says Hey, man, tell it like it was!' He shrugs, spreads his hands. 'Thing is, I'd have been glad to.'

I hand over one of my sheets of paper to him, point to the passage at the top. It's a story from the legend of Fionn.

Fionn asks his followers, 'What is the finest music in the world?' And they give their various answers. The call of a cuckoo. The laughter of a girl. Then they ask Fionn what he thinks. And he answers, the music of what happens. 'Beautiful!' says Neil, handing me back the page.

'I'm writing about MacCaig at the minute,' I tell him. 'He once described himself as a Zen Calvinist!'

'Ha! He won't thank you for that.'

'Listen. Do you fancy a cup of tea?'

'Hey!' he says. 'Is the Pope a Catholic?'

In the tearoom he says, 'Stevenson's your man.'

'Stevenson?'

'Have a look at his "Child's Garden." Then check out a wee book called "Fables." It's the two sides, you see. Innocence and Experience. Here, I'll tell you my favourite one of the fables. This man meets a young lad weeping. And he asks him. What are you weeping for? And the lad says, I'm weeping for my sins. And the man says. You must have little to do. The next day they meet again. And the lad's weeping. And the man asks him. Why are you weeping now? And the lady says, Because I have nothing to eat. And the man says, I thought it would come to that.'

Neil throws back his head and laughs. 'There's Zen Calvinism for you!'

'The Ken Noo school!'

'Lord, Lord we didna ken!'

'Aye, weel, ye ken noo!'

He thumps the table, laughs again.

Over more tea, I find myself telling him about the woman this morning, listening endlessly to *Nessun Dorma.*

'Sad,' he says.

Then I tell him about that dragon I once painted on the wall. And he stares at me.

'Now that is something.'

'How do you mean?'

'There is this Chinese story,' he says. 'About an artist that paints a dragon. And his master tells him he mustn't complete it. He has to leave a wee bit unfinished. The artist says fine, no problem. But sooner or later his curiosity gets the better of him. And he finishes it off. And the dragon comes to life and devours him!'

I stare at him.

'I've never heard that story in my life. How could I have known?'

'We know more than we think,' says Neil. 'I mean everything's telling us, all the time. Only we don't listen.'

'Sure!' For some reason, his story's disurbed me. 'Better get back to my work.'

'The dissertation!' He looks amused.

Outside in the High Street he asks, by the way, how's Mary? And I tell him she's fine, she's away in the States, she'll be back at the end of the week.

'Good,' he says.

We stop at the corner.

'Right.'

'One last thing,' he says. 'Do you know the story of *Turandot*, where your *Nessun Dorma* comes from?'

'Just that it's set in China.'

'Aye.' He nods, grins. 'Check it out sometime. I think you'll find it interesting.'

Back at the library, I find myself looking in the music section, finding the libretto.

An unknown prince arrives at the great Violet City, its gates carved with dragons. In the course of the story, he finds his long-lost father. He solves three riddles which grant him the hand of the Princess Turandot. The answer to one riddle is the name of the princess. The answers to the others are hope and blood.

The word Tao catches my eye as I flick through the pages. The prince is told, *Non esiste che il niente nel quale ti annulli.* There exists only the nothingness in which you annihilate yourself. *Non esiste che il Tao.* There exists only the Tao.

One last passage jumps out at me, a paragraph in the introduction, explaining that Puccini never completed the opera, it was left unfinished when he died.

I see Neil's grin. Everything is telling us. All the time.

I close the book, put it back on the shelf.

When I'd lived four years in that white room with a view, the painted dragon unfinished on the wall, I met Mary and moved out. We travelled a bit, in France, then Italy. We got work teaching English, enough to get by. I sent my father postcards from every new place. When we came back home I went to see him. The flat had come to have the old familiar smell, staleness of booze and fags and no hope. He was listening again to his sad songs. He had lost his job, been laid off. He was months behind with his rent, and we were too broke to bail him out.

In the end he had to give up the flat. I helped him find a bedsit near the university. He liked it well enough, liked the neighbourhood. The bedsit was his home for five years, till he died.

Ten o'clock at night and *Nessun Dorma* still going strong. She's been playing it for 24 hours at least.

At the World Cup, Italia 90, in one of the games Scotland lost, the song was played at half-time, the video shown on a giant screen in the stadium. Someone shouted, 'Easy the big man!' And the whole Scottish crowd started chanting.

> *One Pavarotti*
> *There's only one Pavarotti,*
> Scotland in Europe.
> Wha's like us?

My old neighbour Archie next door has started up on his accordion. He plays it most nights, runs through his repertoire. *Moonlight and Roses, Bridges of Paris, Spanish Eyes.* A taste for the exotic. He plays with gusto, undaunted by the odd bum note. I find it unutterably melancholy.

The long dark night. This wee cold country.

Ach.

I do know the noise has something to do with me as it batters into my awareness, harasses me awake. The phone ringing at 3am. So it must be Mary calling from the States. Still groggy, I pick it up, hear that transatlantic click and hiss, then her voice warm.

Hello?

'Hi.'

I know it's late, sorry.

It's one of those lines. The person speaking drowns out the other. When you talk you hear a faint, delayed echo of your own voice. Not great for communication. Those little phatic responses keep getting lost. So I just listen as she tells me the story. New York's been hit by a hurricane. Roads are flooded, bridges closed, subways off. The airports are shut down, all flights cancelled, no way she can get out.

Sorry.

'So it'll be, what, a few more days?'

Whenever.

I listen to the wash of noise down the line, feel the distance. Then she's telling me about a call she made to the airline, and the woman she spoke to knew nothing about the situation.

So I says, Haven't you been watching the news on TV? And she says, You think I'm sitting here watching TV? I'm working!

I laugh at that, miss the next bit.

. . . and I ask her what I should do, and she says, Stay tuned!

'Nice!'

What?

'I said, Nice!'

Yeah, right.

'So!'

So this is costing.

'Who cares?'

What?

'Never mind!'

I'll call when I know what's happening.

'See you soon.'

Take care.

I put down the phone, stare at it. I shiver and realize I'm chilled from sitting. I know I won't get back to sleep so I pad through to the kitchen, put on the kettle, light the gas fire. Then I hear the commotion out in the street, voices raised, an argument, crackle of an intercom. I pull back the curtain and peer out, see the flashing light on top of the police car.

Two young policemen are at the groundfloor window, trying to reason with the woman, and she's screaming out at them. 'I know the score here! I know what's going on!'

Finally she bangs the window shut. Then the music stops, cuts off.

A man's voice shouts out from an upstairs window. 'Nessun bloody dorma right enough! How's anybody supposed to sleep through this lot?' And he too slams his window.

The car drives off, and everything is quiet again, so quiet. For no reason I get dressed and go out, walk to the end of the street. I stand there a while, looking up at the night sky. The winds are high. The way it looks the clouds stand still, the stars go scudding past. Somewhere a dog barks. A taxi prowls by.

The music of what happens.

Stay tuned.

That groundfloor window is open again, just a fraction. Smell of my father's house. Things left unfinished. The music is playing, one more time, but quietly now, so I have to strain to hear it. I stand there and listen, right to the end.

Vincero.

Nessun Dorma

Discussion Points

Use the following questions as a framework for your thinking and talking about the story. Questions 1–15 are designed to help you explore some of the detail of the story, and questions 16–18 may help you to tie that detail together.

Page 35

1. How would you describe the **mood** created by the first two paragraphs?

2. The dialogue increases the sense of mystery – we are as interested in 'the wifie' as the narrator; but what other feelings does the narrator have?

Page 37

3. 'The room stinks of misery.'

   How does the narrator's description of the room help us to understand this image?

   What important detail do we learn about the narrator in this paragraph?

4. Is our desire to know about the woman satisfied by what she says?

5. 'She finds the remote control and winds back the tape.'

   How does this sentence serve as a link to the next section of the story, where the writer uses **flashback** to take us to his teenage bedroom?

   What is it about the woman's room which might also have reminded the narrator of his past? (Look at the description of colour and smell.)

Page 39

6. 'Princess you too are waking in your cold room.'

   Think about the room in which this piece of music is being played – is there any **irony** in this line?

7. The section of the story takes us further back in the narrator's life; what do we learn about the narrator's father?

Pages 40 and 41

N.B. Zen – one of two main forms of Buddhism in Japan, Zen defies easy definition. Very broadly, it concerns **instinctual** knowing rather than knowing **about** something.

Calvinism – the doctrines of the religious reformer John Calvin greatly influenced Scottish Protestantism.

MacCaig – Norman MacCaig, contemporary Scottish poet.

Stevenson – Robert Louis Stevenson, Scottish writer.

8. What do you understand by 'the music of what happens'?

Page 42

9. Why is the narrator unnerved by the Chinese story?

10. What do you think Neil might mean by 'everything's telling us, all the time'?

Pages 43 and 44

11. Look at the two sections from 'When I'd lived . . . Ach'.

    The writer mingles sadness with humour – how?

12. Look at that final 'Ach'. (page 44)

    What does the writer gain by isolating the word like this?

13. How is the phone call to Mary connected to the rest of the story? (Think about what the story seems to be about.)

Page 46

14. The musical **motif** which runs through the story is used very overtly here – can you pick out some examples and describe their effect?

15. *'Vincero'* means 'I shall win'. Do you think the writer is being **ironic** here, or is this a hopeful ending?

16. Think about the way that **music** is used in the story; and the phrase 'the music of what happens'. How does the idea of music form a link between the woman's life and the narrator's life?

17. The writer frequently refers to stories from other cultures – what might he be saying about the common **purpose** of stories?

18. 'Everything is telling us. All the time.'

    This idea is repeated in the story. What do you think the writer is trying to tell you?

Writing About the Story

It may be that, following your discussion of the story, you wish to explore it further by writing about it. Here are a few points for you to consider, which might help you to clarify your thoughts.

1. It has been said that the best short stories are essentially prose poems – there is nothing gratuitous about them. How does Alan Spence manage to convey ideas to us in a very *concise* way? Think about:

    (a) Imagery
    (b) Dialogue (how do characters reveal themselves?)
    (c) Repetition (do words change in meaning as they are repeated?)
    (d) Stories within stories (how *many* stories are being told?)

Janice Galloway

Janice Galloway was born in Ayrshire where she taught for ten years. Since first publication in 'Edinburgh Review' in 1986, her writing has attracted outstanding acclaim. Her first novel, 'The Trick is to Keep Breathing' (Polygon, 1990) won a Scottish Arts Council Award and the MIND/Allan Lane Award and was shortlisted for the Whitbread First Novel and Scottish First Book of the Year.

One story from the following collection, 'Blood' (Secker, 1992) won the Perrier/Cosmopolitan Prize: the collection itself was shortlisted for the Guardian Fiction Award, Scottish Book of the Year and the People's Prize.

Her second novel 'Foreign Parts' was published by Jonathan Cape. She lives in Glasgow and has one son.

Scenes from the Life No. 26: The Community and the Senior Citizen

A sudden flash, some half-hearted flickering. A three-sided box. It is a compact living room and the chief impression is one of brightness. Yes, a lot of afternoon sunlight is forcing in from somewhere off to the left. It spreads on the pale wallpaper like transparent butter and creates a long rhombus of itself on the carpet; a contained shape from the toomuchness of outside. Much of the floral tracery of the carpet is lost inside it and the pink design is clear only at the fitted extremities. There are no shadows in the corners, only a neat standard lamp with a plain shade, a green wicker chair.

Two very white doors complete the harmony of the composition. They hang as balances on the centre of the facing wall, radiating a high, professional gloss, the more noticeable for their being so close together. On the strip between, some five feet from the white skirting, a square frame reflects fiercely. The picture or photograph behind the glass is almost entirely glared out by bars of light on the surface; but something dark seems to be whispering up through the sheen as of a black-and-white still. We may assume a wedding photograph rather than linger.

On the right, another door, fractionally ajar, and a low table with an empty glass bowl: opposite, near the light source and pale grey curtains, an empty display cabinet. Details obtained by absorption, for our eyes have become used to the decibel level of light and are veering naturally to the main interest in the middle of the room.

Centred squarely toward us is a large, dove-grey settee. A fine stripe shaved into its plain velvet pile makes three sections of the whole and these, in turn, are bisected by the lightshape from the window, washing the left of the settee paler than the right. Just within the shaded part, a solid figure bulks down the cushions, spoiling the symmetry. Swathed in navy blue, it is the only dark thing in the room. The lower buttons of the coat are undone, revealing a wedge of blue skirt and plump orange legs stretching down to flat black shoes. There is a scant navy hat on her short auburn hair, a black shoulder bag resting at one hip. Ah. It is the HEALTH VISITOR. A young woman, her face is full and smooth, her lips ripe and dark from recent applications of warm porcelain; she has been drinking tea. The cup relaxes in one pink palm – the left. The other hand sports a fragment of gingernut biscuit (a pleasing colour halfway between that of her hair and legs) which she waves as she talks. For though we cannot hear, she is talking: her head nods and her mouth moves. The angle of her gaze and that moving mouth prompt a glance in their direction. Yes, there is someone in the companion chair now we look. Feel free; she cannot know we are watching.

It is an OLD WOMAN. Three-quarters in profile, her body conveys an uncomfortable blend of rigidity and exhaustion. Feet and knees brace tightly together, swollen ankles jowling over the lip of her slippers, yet her torso slumps and her neck droops over quite hypothetical breasts. Certainly she is thin; tortuously thin: limbs emerge as skinbound sinew from the hems of her clothes. The clothes themselves, a knitted skirt and top in neutral tones, are dull and undistinguished – flesh colour – though nothing like her own. Her skin is uniformly pale, a waxy cream-yellow without blemish. The hands that for the moment spread from cuff-ends to cover the dove-grey armrests seem painted over, or squeezed into surgical gloves. They seem not to possess fingernails. Her hair is no more reassuring: a frazzle of neglected vanity with pale roots and raggedy red-grey ends sticking up untidily like half-rinsed paintbrushes. Beneath hangs her face, and, more obviously, her mouth. It gapes. And there are silver trails at its corner. Occasionally, she makes a tentative dab at the runnel of saliva, but the sheen seems to vanish only long enough for another thread to form and ooze back along the same path to her chin. The eyes, too, shift continually from side to side, suggesting a nervous or ingrained habit. She has certainly let herself go.

Between the two of them is a low table strewn with tea things – an empty cup and saucer, a second saucer and teaspoon, an opened carton of milk and a blue plate with the remaining gingernut. It seems they have been sitting for some time.

The HEALTH VISITOR stirs. The scent of the room rises – a faint cloy of earth and cold meat we had not noticed before. Now there is a soft scuffling as the HEALTH VISITOR uncrosses her plump legs, the creak of the settee, then the dry click of the cup against the saucer as she sets it down. Someone increases the volume further.

HEALTH VISITOR:	No other visitors tonight then? Just yourself?
OLD WOMAN:	*Silence. Shakes her head and dabs her mouth.*
HEALTH VISITOR:	But everything's fine just the same? Keeping well eh? I say you're keeping well.
OLD WOMAN:	*Silence.*

HEALTH VISITOR:	That's good. All the messages in for the weekend – nothing I can get you?
OLD WOMAN:	*Silence. Nods her head and moves her lips.*
HEALTH VISITOR:	It's good to see you're keeping yourself busy anyway. Keeping busy eh?

Throughout this exchange, the OLD WOMAN has been struggling with her face and now manages to make a slack oblong of her mouth with lips parted and some teeth showing in the divide. Once attained, its maintenance is no easy matter. The grimace is tight, cutting creases into her cheeks and her dribbling is markedly worse. But she holds it there, and through its effortful set dredges up her voice and an answer.

OLD WOMAN:	Try to.
HEALTH VISITOR:	Good for you. Good for you, Mrs Maule. Pity there aren't more like you. Well, we know don't we. It's up to yourself in the last analysis, isn't it?

The HEALTH VISITOR has begun to wrestle up from the settee, clutching her bag, then standing to smooth down the creases and crumbs from the navy coat, restoring her authority. It is a signal. The OLD WOMAN takes it to begin her own procedure for rising, grasping the armrests with whitening knuckles, bracing her feet and pushing, pushing till finally she is erect. And all the while she has managed to support the grim rictus we know for a smile; holds it and strengthens it in triumph though her eyes droop and the muscles quiver. When she stands she is grinning still. The HEALTH VISITOR reddens with relief and satisfaction at her own restraint whilst staging an unconcerned fastening of the lower buttons of her coat. They pause together for a moment, their backs to us, then move slowly around the settee and towards the doors.

HEALTH VISITOR:	Another nice cup of tea, Mrs Maule. Always appreciated.

OLD WOMAN:	*Nods. A low hum of acknowledgement.*
HEALTH VISITOR:	Anything you've forgotten to say to me? Or we haven't talked about yet?
OLD WOMAN:	*Silence.*
HEALTH VISITOR:	And I suppose you won't let me help with the cups this time either? Eh?
OLD WOMAN:	No no. Fine.

This concludes just as they reach the doors and we begin to appreciate the artistry of the HEALTH VISITOR in this professional and crafted leavetaking. It has been tailored for no awkward silences, smoothing her exit for them both. Now she selects the right-hand door of the pair, turns the handle and pushes to reveal a porch beyond. She steps into this bridge between the inner and outer spaces, reaching. The exterior door opens to an immediate balloon of traffic sound, alarmingly loud, and softer, unidentified scuttling. We can see a flap of sky too – a thick triangle of afternoon blue. The HEALTH VISITOR stops, acclimatizing, then turns for her farewells, filling the box of porchway and blocking out the slices of external things. The OLD WOMAN stays safe at her end of the runway.

It is time to speak again.

HEALTH VISITOR:	I'm away then. Cheerio, Mrs Maule. See you next week. Cheerio then. See and look after yourself now.

If the OLD WOMAN speaks, we cannot hear. With a click and a shudder, the noise cuts and the HEALTH VISITOR is gone, leaving a last cheerio trapped in the silence. The OLD WOMAN closes her interior door and stands motionless. A car horn sounds cheerily outside. The OLD WOMAN continues to face the white door. Her shoulders expand and drop. That is all. When she turns we see the harsh stretch has erased from her mouth and her eyelids are shut. She waits, breathing deeply till the tautness in the room breaks down and settles around her feet;

she waits till we feel something has been accomplished. Now we advance.

She begins by clearing the tea things and carrying them off to the room on the right. She nudges the door open enough for us to see inside to a sink, draining board, racks of cleaning materials in bottles. She settles the tray on the stainless drainer then, with a jerky delicacy that suggests distaste, rinses the cups, saucers and single spoon at the cold tap. As each emerges from the water, she drops it into a red plastic bin at her foot. The washing cloth follows, then, unrinsed, the blue plate and its remaining biscuit. The bin swallows them whole, snaps shut. She wipes her hands against her skirt, reaches and opens the white kitchen unit above the sink. It is scrupulously empty, save in one blushing corner where a red packet flops untidily. The bin accepts this too and the cupboard is clean.

The milk carton is waiting. She takes it from the tray and tips the last of it down the sink, erasing white stains with swirling water. But the determined vigour of her performance begins to tell, for her breathing is audible and she is bracing her arms straight, supporting herself at the edge of the sink. She increases the flow of the tap, masking the sound of her working lungs, but the beating rise and fall of her frail chest seems to worsen. Her head droops, eyes stare: something worming in her throat forces her mouth wide in a retch. The coursing of the water exaggerates deafeningly: we feel the cold scent of steel and the pulsing at her temples – reaching to know what is wrong. Some of us go further. For now the flickering comes again and – single frames of something, flashing too quickly, a confused mesh of images, unkent things, disconnected pieces.

There is the OLD WOMAN *standing at a full-length mirror in a too-thin nightdress, feeling at her hips through the cloth; now her face at a magnifying mirror, bloated and salivating: a white lavatory bowl darkening with regurgitated matter: a still glass of clear fluid and a clock: a jumble of bones weeping on a bedspread vomiting.*

But this is revolting. Our empathy snaps back. A thick whiff of nausea, a blink or two, and we are relieved to find the shock has jolted us out of the kitchen and back to our vantage point in the living room. There, reassuringly on the right again, is the OLD WOMAN buttressed at the sink. She recovers in her own time, turns off the tap, straightens her face to the slack-jawed norm. She is coming out – perhaps we should go.

But one door still retains its secret. It radiates whitely from the back of the room. Curiosity makes us stay as she crosses the floor and enters through it, though she closes the blank panel on us almost immediately. A little aural concentration will do: whistling taps, pounding water obligingly reveal an off-stage bath. Soon, the sounds of its filling accede to the shuffle of resettling liquid and some coy splashes. Still, it does not do to be too interested; we have learned that from experience. We deflect attention to an idle re-examination of the living room, its pale colours and lightweight furnishings. The diminished rhombus of sunlight on the settee and the carpet shows some time has elapsed. The shifting music of bathing plays from behind the closed door, and, with the monotony of the surroundings, does much to restore serenity. Perhaps we begin to doze. For it is not till the draining gurgle from the bathroom and damp scuffling of the OLD WOMAN's towel that we notice the box, halfway up the wall next to the lamp. At first glance, it passed for a telephone, but now shows something smaller. There is no receiver. It takes some narrowing of the eyes before we see the switch and the muzzle of an intercom. The box and the surroundings click. This is a sheltered house. Behind this box, in some other place, another living room, is a listener: a caretaker elsewhere, yet securely here in representational plastic. Ah. A little weight drops from our necks.

It is all more containable now, and we can afford a little sentimental soft-focus as she appears at the bathroom door, through a spill of mist, in a white dressing-gown: an angel in an aura of condensation. Her hair has frizzled out fetchingly with steam and combing, to a frail red and white netting about her skull. Her face is pink, fuller; pretty with rubbing and the heat. And now she moves, her co-ordination seems easier, as though the invisible bath has oiled the joints to suppleness. More marvellous still are her eyes. Something in the hot-water clouds has freed their colour. They are large, wider: an unnaturally lucid azure. It flashes from under the lids as she turns her head left to right, right to left 180° and back; electric blue pulses from a cardiograph. Satisfied, she crosses the room to the window. She draws the blind, cutting the lifeline of the light shape on the floor, and the room relaxes into matching shades of grey. The glare on the wall-mounted photograph, too, drops with a blink, attracting attention. She approaches, looks, touches once. When she turns, we see her rest one fingertip vertically against the flat lines of her lips: *does not equal.* Then, soundlessly, she stretches her hands to the ceiling, fingers in fans and arms at full reach. They pull away from her till the striving burns: a whimper of pain breaks her concentration. Enough.

Something begins. Some timetable sets in motion with her firm, fluid movements. Her meticulousness suggests planning; preparations made for a specific moment, and, despite our intrusion, the moment is come. She has no need to seize – her grasp is assured. We are too far and at the wrong angle to read her expression with any degree of accuracy, but the set of body, calm manner and miraculously closed mouth show eagerness, excitement. It seems inappropriate now to cast her as the OLD WOMAN – we must search for another name. Was it . . . yes – it is MRS MAULE. This is MRS MAULE setting her home to rights.

Already, she has moved the armchair away, off to the right. As she rolls aside the settee, a flat, brown packet appears on the carpet in the space it vacates. The centre of the room is a newly-cleared stage with this single prop. She plumps the settee cushions, erasing the cooled hollow that held her recent guest (now visiting health upon others, elsewhere, with different cup warming her hand) before collecting the rest. First the coffee table, lifted and centred in the thicket of woven flowers, the surface dusted with one cuff. Now, the packet, laid accurately straight along one edge of the table-top. It is an unremarkable packet, just brown paper with a serrated lip.

To the bathroom next, leaving the door wide. She lifts an orderly pile of fleshy things – the discarded clothes – and drops them into a wicker basket; straightens the bathmat and the towels. There is a small white cabinet above the sink, and two shelves inside ranged with bright bottles, boxes and tins. She pushes her hand among the colours to select a tiny brown jar, then closes the cabinet and the room. They have served their purpose.

Only the kitchen door remains. She wades patiently across and enters, alone. The rattle of a blind, whine of the tap, then she surfaces with a tall glass and a bottle of lemonade. A little awkwardly, she manages to fasten this door too, sealing the interior. The set is ready.

MRS MAULE reaches the coffee table to settle the bottle, glass and pill jar in a neat row along the edge of the bag. She opens the lemonade bottle, then kneels upright behind the table and the row of instruments to fill the glass with sizzling liquid. A pearl-string of bubbles, shiny in the half-light, marks a level a few inches from the rim. The rejected bottle sits open on the floor. For a moment or two, she stares intently at the brown bag before picking it up, gently, with both hands to spill its filling over the table-top. A scatter of paper – several sheets in fresh to faded shades of white. One after the other, she lifts and presses these flat, building a tidy pile. Each surface spreads in turn under her fingers, some showing heavily-typed faces, some showing nothing. It takes a little time. MRS MAULE glares hard at her work, her hands resting on the edges of the sheets. It is difficult to discern where the paper stops and the flesh begins, for the light is very dim now and the blood that quickened in the bath is slowing, drawing colour as it cools. Her face is settling as she sits, creases returning where warmth leaves. It deepens as we watch: she is making us wait. Second after second – almost five minutes. It would be easy to let attention wander, cast around the room, but where is there to see? It is neat, drab, orderly. All that moves are the silver beads in the lemonade, shushing a silence from the top of the glass.

It concludes at last. She gathers animation slowly, first opening the pill jar to pour out the contents, a straggle of yellow tablets across her papers. She discards the bottle and turns to the glass, raising it in her left hand. The rest is brisk and decisive. It is a routine. It works like this:

1. A couple of tablets in the right hand;

2. Sip;

3. Insert the pills between the lips;

4. Snap down;

5. Sip;

6. Swallow.

Each cycle ends with a pause, sometimes a curling of the lip – then begins again. And with greater or lesser pauses, greater or lesser doses of the yellow tablets, she absorbs the whole cache. It takes about four minutes in all, not a long performance, and manages to retain interest throughout. At the end, at least half the lemonade remains in the glass, but the waste is immaterial and she pushes it to one side of the table. Her small weight shifts one hip, freeing her legs to stretch out in stages. Then manoeuvering lumpily on her elbows, she lowers her back, lying flat on the carpet. She is staring at the ceiling. One hand is restless at her side. It twitches until she accedes to its need. Her gaze does not flinch as she lets it become a thing apart; rising to pluck at the candlewick belt, slipping inside the border of her grown. It fumbles there under the cloth, stroking at one hidden breast. A caress. Soon, she is still again. We notice the crook of her elbow is dry and bulbous: the bath-plumped tissue deflated, unattractively aged once more. Within the waxy face, her eyes keep searching the ceiling. Let her wait on. We have other things to do.

Scenes from the Life No. 26: The Community and the Senior Citizen

Discussion Points

Use the following questions as a framework for your thinking and talking about the story. Questions 1–25 are designed to help you explore some of the detail of the story, and questions 26–30 may help you to tie that detail together.

Page 51

1. Why is the room described as a 'three-sided box'?

2. What do you understand by 'the toomuchness of outside'?

Page 52

3. Why are the words 'HEALTH VISITOR' and 'OLD WOMAN' in block capital letters?

4. What is the effect of 'she cannot know we are watching'?

5. What does the description of the Old Woman convey to you? Do you think any **irony** is intended in *'She has certainly let herself go'*?

Pages 54 and 55

6. What does the dialogue suggest about the Health Visitor's attitude to the Old Woman?

Page 55

7. What is the **tone** of 'we begin to appreciate the artistry of the Health Visitor in this professional and crafted leavetaking'?

8. Look at the description of the physical change in the old

woman when the Health Visitor has left – what does it suggest to you about how the Old Woman feels?

Pages 56 and 57

9. The Old Woman's tidying up is unusual – what does it suggest?

10. Look at the section in italics – what does it convey to you? (What is the effect of 'a jumble of bones'?)

11. What is it that is 'revolting'?

   What is it that the writer is suggesting about 'our empathy'?

12. Is there any **irony** in 'This is a sheltered house'?

Pages 57 and 58

13. Look at the description of the Old Woman after her bath – apart from an angel, does she remind you of anything else?

14. What is it, do you think, that the Old Woman is reaching for, striving for?

15. What do you think 'does not equal' means?

16. Why is it 'inappropriate now to cast her as the OLD WOMAN'?

Pages 58 and 59

17. Comment on 'now visiting health upon others'.

18. Why is the flat packet *hidden* under the settee? (Why would anyone hide something in their own home?)

19. Comment on 'the set is ready'.

20. What do you think might be in the packet?

Pages 59 and 60

21. What is the effect of the list of the woman's actions?

22. 'Cache' usually suggests treasure of some sort – how appropriate is the word in this context?

23. What does 'the waste is immaterial' suggest about how the woman lived her life?

24. What is the effect of making the phrase 'A caress' into a 'sentence'?

25. 'We have other things to do.' What does this suggest about us?

26. Think about the use of theatrical terminology in this story – why do you think the writer has chosen to blend drama and narrative in this way?

27. What is it that the writer is saying about the way we treat our old people?

28. 'It's up to yourself in the last analysis, isn't it?'

    The Health Visitor says this unthinkingly, as a cliché; but what is its effect, in the context of the story?

29. Would you say that the manner of the woman's death was sad?

30. How would you describe the **tone** of the story?

Writing About the Story

It may be that, following your discussion of the story, you wish to explore it further by writing about it. Here are a few points for you to consider, which might help you to clarify your thoughts.

1. '. . . ways people behave when they think they are all alone and nobody's looking at them, that's the kind of thing I want to write about.'

Janice Galloway

Although we never hear the Old Woman's voice, by the end of the story we have a very clear idea of the kind of person she is. How does Janice Galloway develop the character in the story? You might want to think about:

(a) The use of stereotypes, and the way the character breaks through our expectations of her.
(b) The use of some of the conventions of drama – how are we encouraged to 'see' the woman?
(c) The **pace** of the story – there is a sense of mounting tension as the woman prepares for death. How is this created?

Further Reading

Perhaps you feel like reading some other works by Scottish writers – why not try some of these?

'The Sound of my Voice' (Canongate)
Ron Butlin's novel is a sensitive portrayal of a man experiencing breakdown – of his job, his family, himself. Simply told and very readable.

'The Missionary' (Polygon)
In this novel **Alex Cathcart** explores the lives of two men – James Black who is on his way down, and David Parks, on his way up – within the context of modern Christianity. Energetic and unstoppable.

'The Killjoy' (Black Swan)
Anne Fine is better known as a children's writer, but in this adult novel she has produced a very chilling tale of an obsessive and destructive passion. Not for the fainthearted.

'Poor Things'
If you liked the idea of Frankenstein's monster, you'll love this. **Alisdair Gray's** fast and funny novel set at the turn of the century follows the life of the mysterious Bella Baxter – a beauty, or a monster? Read on . . .

'A Disaffection' (Secker & Warburg)
You've probably heard of **James Kelman** – he is fast becoming known as the voice of working-class Scotland. This novel looks at one week in the life of Patrick Doyle, a young teacher in a comprehensive school. Angry and funny.

'Looking for the Possible Dance'
A.L. Kennedy is a young Scottish writer with a growing reputation for excellence. This novel explores an area familiar to us all – the search for love and the difficulty of connection. Beautiful and haunting.

'Stone Over Water'

Carl MacDougall's novel uses a twin-story format to tell us the story of Angus, an orphan who is adopted at twelve by the foster family from Hell. Not the easiest of reads, but well worth the effort.

'The Great Profundo and other stories'

This is a bit of a cheat – **Bernard MacLaverty** is technically Irish, but has been living and writing in Scotland for years, and these stories are really just too good to miss.

And for those of you who enjoy poetry, why not go to a library immediately and delve into the works of . . .

Douglas Dunn	Alison Fell	Kathleen Jamie
Jackie Kay	Tom Leonard	Liz Lochhead
Norman MacCaig	Stephen Mulrine	Edwin Morgan